I'm Reading About

MOUNT RUSHMORE

GALLOPADE

by Carole Marsh

Printed and Manufactured in Peachtree City, GA., USA www.gallopade.com

Book design: Susan Van Denhende

Editor: Janice Baker

Photo Credits: Cover: Audrey M Vasey/Bigstock.com. Page 3: Robert Voight/Bigstock.com. Page 5: iofoto.com/Bigstock.com. Page 9: 9A: Rise Studios, National Park Service; 9B: Harris & Ewing, Library of Congress. Page 11: Washington: Rembrandt Peale, Google Cultural Institute; Jefferson: Rembrandt Peale, White House Historical Association; Roosevelt: Pach Brothers, Library of Congress; Lincoln: Alexander Gardner, www.britannica.com. Page 13: Library of Congress. Page 15: National Park Service. Page 17: Charles D'Emery, National Park Service. Page 18: Lincoln Borglum, National Park Service. Page 20: Rise Studios, National Park Service. Page 22: National Park Service. Page 24: Vern Faber/Bigstock.com. Page 26A: jkraft5/Bigstock.com; 26B,C,D: National Park Service. Page 28A: The Final Model of Mt. Rushmore in the sculptor's studio by Aaron Vowels, CC BY 2.0; 28B: National Park Service. Page 30: http://archive.cyark.org/perspective-of-abraham-lincoln-created-from-laser-scan-data-1-mediabyCDDV/CyArk CC BY-SA 1.0. Page 32A&D: jkraft5/Bigstock.com; 32B: National Park Service; 32C: Montanaw/Bigstock.com. Page 34: Olivier/Bigstock.com.

Mount Rushmore
is a great place to visit!

What is so special about
Mount Rushmore?

Let's read about it and see!

INTRODUCTION

Mount Rushmore National Memorial is a huge sculpture carved into a mountain.

The sculpture shows the faces of four U.S. Presidents:

- George Washington
- Thomas Jefferson
- Theodore Roosevelt
- Abraham Lincoln

The presidents represent the first 150 years of U.S. history.

Mount Rushmore

LOCATION

Mount Rushmore is located
in the Black Hills of South Dakota.
South Dakota's nickname is
"The Mount Rushmore State."

South Dakota became a state in 1889.
It was the 40th state to join
the United States of America!

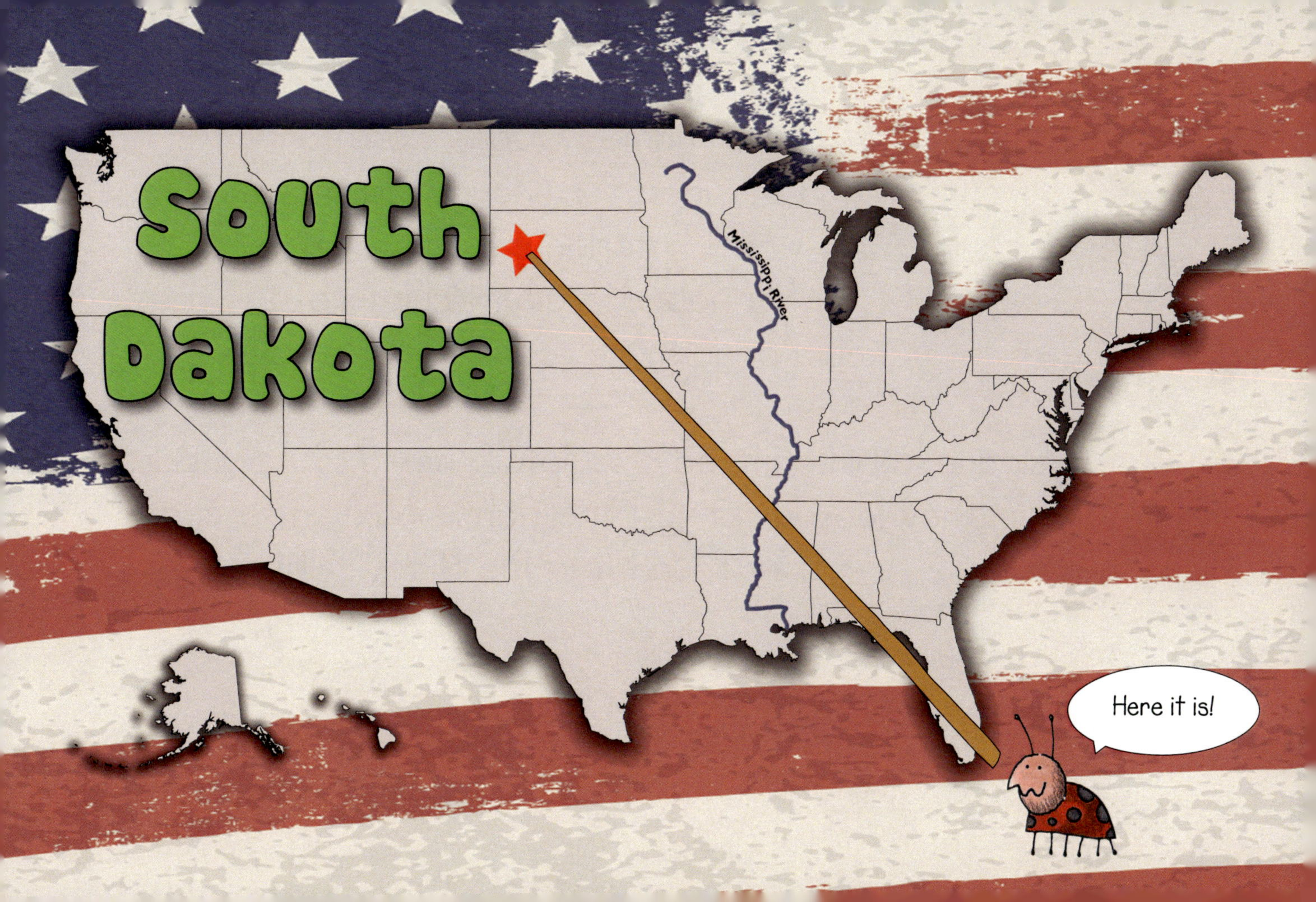
South Dakota
Mississippi River
Here it is!

IDEA

A man named Doane Robinson
had the idea for Mount Rushmore.
He was a historian in South Dakota.
He hoped a giant sculpture
would bring more tourists to the state.

Doane Robinson hired a sculptor named Gutzon Borglum.
They looked for just the right mountain to carve.
They found it in the Black Hills!

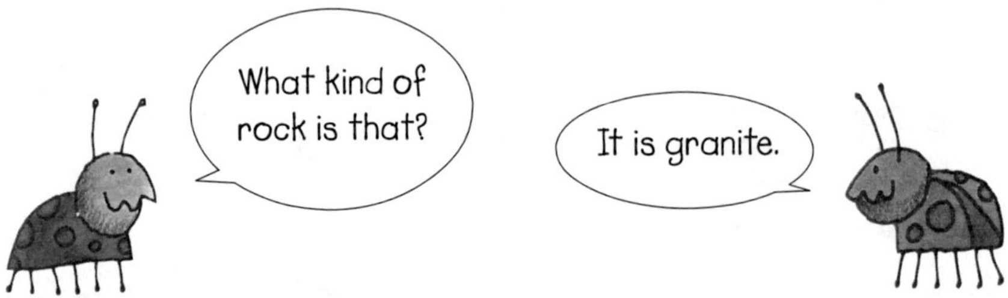

Mountain before Carving

Gutzon Borglum

PRESIDENTS

The four Presidents on Mount Rushmore represent the birth, growth, development, and preservation of the United States of America.

- George Washington – birth of a new nation
- Thomas Jefferson – growth through the Louisiana Purchase
- Theodore Roosevelt – economic growth in early 1900s
- Abraham Lincoln – preservation through the Civil War

The Louisiana Purchase doubled the size of the United States!

Four Presidents

George Washington
1st President

Thomas Jefferson
3rd President

Theodore Roosevelt
26th President

Abraham Lincoln
16th President

MODEL

To create his sculpture, Borglum made a plaster model.
One inch on his model was equal to
one foot on the mountain.

At first, Borglum planned to sculpt the Presidents
from the waist up.
However, he ended up just creating their heads.

Sculpture Model
Gutzon Borglum's Model
of Mt. Rushmore Memori
Washington, Jefferson
Roosevelt & Lincoln
©
-RISE STUDIO-

WORKERS

Work began to create Mount Rushmore in 1927.
Borglum hired about 400 people to help him.

He needed people to build roads.
He needed people to blast rock from the mountain.
He needed people to hoist workers up and down.
He needed people to sharpen drill bits...and more!

Work stopped in the winter.
It was just too COLD!

Jobs to Do

Hoisting workers

Sharpening drill bits

Preparing dynamite
DU PONT

WORKERS

Working on Mount Rushmore was a dangerous job!
Workers dealt with dizzying heights,
dynamite blasts, and extreme weather.

A winch system hoisted workers up and down the mountain.
A winch is a device used for pulling or lifting.
Workers sat in a seat known as a "bosun chair."
Thick steel cables supported the workers
along the mountain's face.

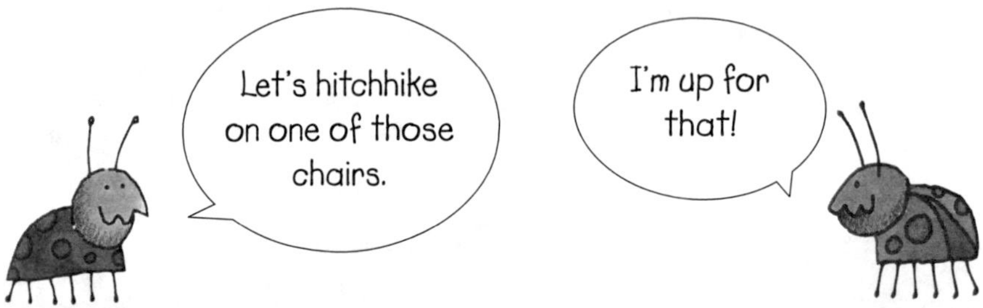

Bosun Chairs

Dynamite

Honeycombing

DYNAMITE

BOOM!

Big blasts of dynamite removed big chunks of rock.
This process carved 90 percent of Mount Rushmore.

Next, workers drilled holes in the mountain.
This process was called "honeycombing."

Then, workers used chisels and hammers
to chip away the rock between the holes.

Finally, workers used a special drill
to smooth out the finished surface.

Colossal Carving

BY THE NUMBERS

Mount Rushmore is HUGE!

- Each head is 60 feet tall.
- The Presidents' eyes are 11 feet across.
- Their noses are 20 feet long.
- Their mouths are 18 feet wide!

Four men on a mountainside
fill us all with American pride!

Father and Son

FAMILY TIES

Carving Mount Rushmore took 14 years—
from 1927 to 1941.
Sadly, Gutzon Borglum died before it was finished.

The good news is his son Lincoln
had been working with him for years.
Lincoln took over and finished the majestic memorial.
Gutzon Borglum would have been proud!

Avenue of Flags

THINGS TO SEE

Greetings! I am the Avenue of Flags.
I am one of the many things to see at Mount Rushmore.
I lead visitors to the Grand View Terrace
and Presidential Trail
for a spectacular view of Mount Rushmore!

I am decorated with 56 colorful flags.
That's one for each state and the six U.S. territories.

Fly your flag high!
Let your state's colors
fill the sky!

Lincoln Borglum Museum
50 LBS
DUPONT EXPLOSIVES
SPECIAL GELATIN
40 % STRENGTH
DUPONT EXPLOSIVES
SPECIAL GELATIN
40 % STRENGTH

I am the Lincoln Borglum Museum.
What can you find here?
Fascinating Mount Rushmore artifacts!

Here are a few examples:

- Masks used to create the sculpture
- Dynamite boxes and blasters
- A winch used to move workers up and down
- Incredible photographs...and more!

Sculptor's Studio

THINGS TO SEE

I am the Sculptor's Studio.
This is where Gutzon Borglum
worked on his models for Mount Rushmore.

Borglum selected the studio's location
so he could have a full view of the mountainside.
Here you can see his models and sculpting tools.
I am so lucky—I got to watch the artist at work!

The Sculptor's Studio is open
from May to September.

Protecting the Memorial

PRESERVATION

Mount Rushmore is pounded by heat, cold, wind, and rain every day of the year. Because of that, the National Park Service takes very good care of this special mountain!

- Workers apply sealants to keep water out of cracks.
- Special sensors monitor the granite for movement.
- Digital scanners record every tiny detail of the faces.

Amazing Memorial

DID YOU KNOW?

Read more fascinating facts about Mount Rushmore!

- Workers earned $8 per day.
- Workers climbed over 500 stairs each day to start work.
- Mountain goats like to climb around the Presidents' heads.
- Over 800 million pounds of rock was blasted off the mountain.
- Mount Rushmore is South Dakota's top tourist attraction!

Mount Rushmore

QUOTE

"Hence, let us place there, carved high, as close to heaven as we can, the works of our leaders, their faces, to show posterity what manner of men they were. Then breathe a prayer that these records will endure until the wind and the rain alone shall wear them away."

– Gutzon Borglum

GLOSSARY

artifact: an object made or used by humans long ago

economic growth: increase in the value of goods and services produced by an economy

historian: a person who writes about or studies history

plaster: a paste that hardens when it dries

posterity: all future generations of people

preservation: to keep or save from injury, loss, or ruin

sculpture: a work of art made by carving or molding clay, stone, metal, etc.

winch: machine with one or more drums on which a rope, cable, or chain is coiled for hauling or hoisting